Peoples and Nations of the

FAR EAST & PACIFIC

A short history of each country in the Far East, Australasia, and the Pacific and Indian Oceans

Sheila Fairfield

Gareth Stevens Publishing
Milwaukee

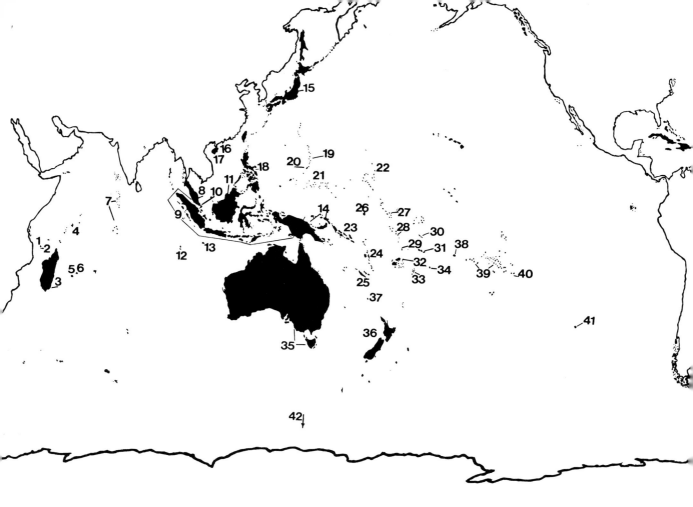

This North American edition first published in 1988 by

Gareth Stevens, Inc.
7317 West Green Tree Road
Milwaukee, Wisconsin 53223, USA

Designed by Behram Kapadia
Individual country maps by Mark Wojcicki
Full-continent map by Kate Kriege
Picture research by Sara Steel

1 2 3 4 5 6 7 8 9 94 93 92 91 90 89 88

Library of Congress Cataloging-in-Publication Data

Fairfield, Sheila.
  Peoples and nations of the Far East and Pacific.

  (Peoples and nations)
  Includes index.
  Summary: Presents a brief history of each country
in the Far East, Australasia, and the Pacific and
Indian Oceans.
  1. East Asia—History—Juvenile literature.
2. Pacific Area—History—Juvenile literature.
I. Title. II. Series: Fairfield, Sheila. Peoples
and nations.
DS511.F29 1988   909'.09823   88-42918
ISBN 1-55532-907-1

CONTENTS

A note on the entries in this book: Each nation-state and dependency has a written entry and its own map or a reference to a map elsewhere in the book. Also, some countries include lands that are geographically separated from the main area. These lands do not have a separate entry but are included in the main country's entry. Finally, some countries are mentioned that are part of other continents. They do not have entries here, but you can find them in other volumes of the *Peoples and Nations* series. Some Asian countries in the Far East have their entries in **Peoples and Nations of Asia**.

MALAYSIA

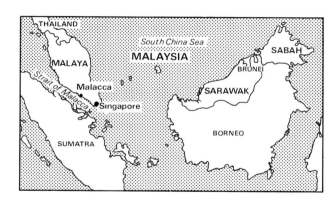

Malaysia is made up of several regions on either side of the South China Sea. On the east are the states of Sarawak and Sabah, on the northern coast of Borneo. On the west is Malaya, now called Peninsular Malaysia because it is on the southern end of a long peninsula. These areas now make up Malaysia. But until 1963, they were independent of one another.

Because Malaya never had good land for growing food, few people lived there. The Malay people lived in tiny states, many of which had to pay taxes to outside countries. There were foreign settlements in Malaya, too, and by AD 300 Indian merchants and Hindu priests lived on the coast.

After 1400 the town of Malacca became a major port. It began as a trading base for pirates and became strong enough to force ships passing through the Strait of Malacca to pay a tax. By 1500 Malacca had become rich and the center of a strong state. Malacca controlled the strait and the sea trade from the spice-growing islands farther east.

Indian and Chinese merchants lived there, and the Indians brought with them a new religion, Islam. This new population got its food from Java, in Indonesia. Many Javanese also lived in Malacca.

In 1500 Malacca was thriving. But it did not thrive for long. Indonesian cities, other states of Malaya, and European traders all fought to control the Strait. Outsiders also tried to take control of the valuable tin mines inside Malaya. By 1511 Malacca had been conquered.

Two groups moved in from Indonesia during the seventeenth century. The Minangkabau, from Sumatra, set up large colonies in south Malaya and then spread up the peninsula. The Bugis from Sulawesi came as pirates. They fought the Malays, the Europeans, and the Minangkabau for control of the tin. By about 1730 they were powerful, and they went on to become Malaya's strongest people.

Among the Europeans seeking trade in the Far East were the British. In 1786 a

On the left, tea and vegetables grow on the steep, terraced hillsides of the Cameron Highlands.

Female workers in a palm oil plantation. The palm oil tree came originally from Africa and has many uses.

British merchant company was on an island off Malaya. By the early nineteenth century, they had founded trading settlements along the Strait of Malacca. The most important was Singapore, founded in 1819. It was a free port. This meant that traders could ship their goods into and out of Singapore without paying special taxes. Singapore quickly attracted shipping. But pirates continued to be a problem along the strait and disrupted trade throughout the region.

The worst pirates were based on Borneo's northern coast. In 1839 an Englishman, James Brooke, settled in Borneo and began to stamp out piracy. He was so successful that he was made ruler of Sarawak in 1846. In the same year the British began to use the island of Labuan, off Borneo's coast, as a coal station for steamships. A British merchant company later bought the area, later called North Borneo. That area and Labuan together made up Sabah.

The people of Borneo were then tribal. They hunted for food or fished or cleared small patches of forest to grow crops. Around the coast lived the Sea Dyaks, a group that included pirates. Also on the coast were towns and trading places where many people of foreign stock lived, including Malays.

Malaya had also begun to attract many Chinese. Businessmen settled in Singapore; miners came to the tin mines. The miners caused so many fights that the Malay rulers asked the British to help keep order. British government workers came to organize the state governments of Malaya. British busi-

nessmen came to Singapore and to inland Malaya, where they set up rubber plantations that employed Indian workers.

By 1948 Sarawak and Sabah, in Borneo, were British colonies, as were Singapore and other British trading settlements in Malaya. Malaya had many rulers, all running their states with British advice.

In that same year a rebellion took place in Malaya. The rebels were communist and Chinese. Many Malays felt the Chinese were a source of trouble, so when Malaya became independent in 1957, it was decided that Singapore, with its mainly Chinese population, should be left out of the new state. In 1963 many felt that Singapore could be allowed in, if there were enough non-Chinese to keep the balance. Malaysia was formed, including Sarawak and Sabah with their Malay, Iban, and Dyak people. Despite this attempt to create a balance among the many racial and ethnic groups, problems persisted. Singapore left Malaysia in 1965 to become an independent nation.

A British force goes up the Perak River to fight against Malay chiefs in 1876.

In the picture on the left the woman is "tapping" a rubber tree. She is cutting the bark so that the sap flows into the collecting jar.

NAURU

Nauru is the only country in the Pacific Ocean that is just one island. All the others are groups of islands.

Nauru is surrounded by a coral reef. It lies in the central Pacific, west of the Gilbert Islands. The Gilbert Islands are in the island nation of Kiribati.

Nauru is tiny, only 8 square miles (21 sq km). There is only a narrow coastal belt of fertile land, where the people live. Inland is a plateau made of rock.

The people are Micronesian, like the people of the Gilbert Islands. They have their own language. They work the fertile land and its crop of coconut trees, fish in the open sea, and raise fish in an inland lagoon.

In 1798 Britain came upon Nauru. But the island was visited by few European ships, most of them whalers, until later in the nineteenth century, when Germany, Britain, and France became powerful in the Pacific. These nations set up plantations to grow crops for trade. They also wanted coal stations for their steamships.

In 1888 Nauru became part of an area that was ruled by Germany. Under German rule, a discovery was made that changed the people's lives forever. They found that the inland plateau was made of phosphate, a valuable fertilizer.

This is how the phosphate was made: The island had always been a stopping place for sea birds. They had landed there for thousands of years, until the ground was deep in bird droppings. Droppings, called

The surface of one of the phosphate mines that have made Nauruans rich.

guano, contain phosphates. Over time, a movement on the ocean bed caused the land to sink. Seawater dissolved the guano and let the phosphate out. The phosphate settled, and when the land rose again it was still there, hardened into rock.

Besides being a valuable fertilizer, phosphate is also used in manufacturing. The newly colonized countries in the South Pacific — Australia and New Zealand — were farming countries. They needed fertilizer. Phosphate mining started on Nauru, and it paid well.

After Germany lost Nauru during World War I (1914-18), the island was ruled by Britain, Australia, and New Zealand. By 1942 about 1,800 Nauruan people lived on the island. So did hundreds of foreign workers, including Chinese, Japanese, British, New Zealanders, Australians, and Pacific Islanders.

In 1942, during World War II, Japan invaded Nauru. About 1,200 Nauruans died. At the end of the war many feared that the Nauruans would die out.

After 1947 Australia controlled Nauru and its phosphates. The people did not die out. They survived — but only to discover that their land was being taken away from them by mining.

Phosphate provided the island's only income. It could not last forever — not beyond the end of the century. The people had to decide what to do when the phosphate was all gone, and their land with it. They could use the profits to buy another island, or they could stay and try to find a new way of living. One thing seemed clear: their bigger, mixed population could not go back to the ways of their ancestors.

Nauru became independent in 1968. Today, the people want to stay. They have built up shipping and other industries to replace phosphate mining. About half the modern population is of Nauruan descent, and both English and Nauruan are the main languages. (See map on page 30.)

WESTERN SAMOA

Western Samoa is an independent country occupying the western islands of the Samoan group. (The smaller group of eastern islands is American Samoa.)

Western Samoa has 1,093 square miles (2,831 sq km) of land. The inhabited islands are Savai'i and Upolu, which are large, and Manono and Apolima, which are small. Both large islands have rugged mountains, and all the islands are volcanic, with much wasteland that has been swept by flows of volcanic lava.

The Samoan islands were settled by about AD 300. Traveling by canoe, the settlers came across the Pacific from eastern Asia. When they had settled in Samoa, they developed a culture and society that are found throughout the south and east Pacific. This culture is now called Polynesian, "from many islands."

Samoa provided the settlers with fertile land, water, and a good climate. There was no need to struggle for survival, so the Samoans had energy to spend on a complicated set of rules for their society. Both the paramount chief, the Tui Manu'a, and the royal families of the various islands were said to be descended from gods. The family was the most important group in Samoan society, and much rivalry existed among the many different island and family groups.

The first European settlers came in about 1845. Catholic missionaries came from France, and traders came from Germany.

The Europeans admired the Samoans, and the Samoans were anxious to sell land and produce to the Europeans. People from the United States also came to buy land for plantations.

Soon there were so many foreigners owning land that Samoa had become a different place. Rival families were fighting over who should be paramount chief. In 1873 the quarreling stopped for a while, and a council of chiefs was set up instead of one ruler. But even the council's powers were limited because its plan for a new Samoan government had to be one that foreign landowners would accept. In the end, the new system was drawn up by an American.

It was not the United States, however, but Germany that first took control. Samoa became a German colony in 1884. But the quarrels among Samoan families grew worse, and civil war broke out. Different foreign powers made things worse by supporting different sides.

In 1899, Germany, Britain, and the United States tried to arrange a solution. They managed to stop the fighting, but Samoa was divided. Germany was to rule western Samoa, and the United States the eastern part.

German rule in western Samoa lasted until World War I (1914-18). Samoa had become rich and European in character.

Samoa is a modern and developed nation, but it does not forget its past. Here two young people on the island of Upolu perform a traditional dance.

The Europeans brought in foreign laborers from China and the western Pacific to work the coconut and cocoa plantations.

In 1914 western Samoa passed to New Zealand. The New Zealanders had to manage Samoans, Germans, other Europeans, foreign workers, and people who were half-Samoan and half-European. This would have been hard enough on its own, but during an epidemic in 1918 many people died. The period of New Zealand's rule was difficult, so Samoa again asked for self-government. This was done in stages, and full independence came in 1962.

There are now about 157 thousand people in Western Samoa; most of them live on Upolu. (See map on page 30.)

MAURITIUS

Mauritius is an independent country that lies in the Indian Ocean, about 500 miles (800 km) east of Madagascar. Its two main islands are Mauritius and Rodriguez islands. Tiny Agalega and St. Brandon islands also belong to Mauritius.

Mauritius is fertile, with volcanic mountains in the south. In the north is a plain, where most of the towns are. Mauritius is small (720 square miles, 1,865 sq km) but about a million people live there.

Mauritius was probably explored by Arabs no later than the tenth century and Malays in the fifteenth century. The Portuguese visited Mauritius around 1510, and in 1598 the Dutch became the first to occupy Mauritius. At that time no people lived there, and the Dutch called it Mauritius after their ruler, Maurice. For years pirates used

the islands as a base, and no lasting settlements were set up until 1721.

In that year a French merchant company founded the capital city as a trading port. The French called it Port Louis, after the French king. At that time all ships from Europe traveled to India and the east by sailing around the southern tip of Africa and then sailing northeast across the Indian Ocean. Mauritius lay on this route. The French gradually built up Port Louis into a major naval base and a useful stopping place for all shipping in the Indian Ocean.

French settlers brought in slaves from East Africa and Madagascar. Soon the main

languages were French and Creole, a mixture of French and African dialects. The French set up Roman Catholic missions and brought in French law.

By the nineteenth century, British merchants had become powerful in India. They could not afford to have the hostile French in control of Port Louis on the sea route from Britain to India, and in 1810, while at war with France, Britain took Mauritius.

The British used the fertile land to grow valuable sugar crops for export. The people, on the whole, kept French and Creole speech, French law, and the Roman Catholic religion. But business life was changed completely by the needs of the sugar plantations. By 1835 slavery had ended and paid workers were needed. The British brought them in from India. Because the Indians increased in number so quickly, clashes broke out between them and the former slaves.

In 1869 the Suez Canal was opened in Egypt. Ships from Europe traveled through the Canal from the Mediterranean to the Red Sea and on to India, across the northern part of the Indian Ocean. They no longer went by way of Mauritius, and Port Louis lost much of its business. Mauritius soon became dependent on sugar. This was fine when prices were high, but when they dropped the economy suffered.

Mauritius became independent in 1968. Sugar is still the main product, but the people also grow tea. The Indians now form the largest group in a population that is ethnically and racially diverse. Of religious groups, the largest is Hindu, followed by Roman Catholics and then Muslims. English is the official language, but many people speak Indian languages, French, and Creole. (See map on page 18.)

Tea is an important crop in Mauritius. Here the rows of tea bushes stretch into the distance in one of the country's many tea gardens.

VANUATU

Vanuatu is a long line of islands in the southwestern Pacific. About eighty islands stretch out over 400 miles (644 km) from northwest to southeast. The largest are Espiritu Santo, Malekula, Aoba, Ambrym, Aurora, and Pentecost.

The climate is hot, but cooling winds blow in from the ocean. The islands are fertile, and their varied landscapes include rocky mountains, plateaus, and rounded hills. Three islands have active volcanoes. Vanuatu is sometimes rocked by earth tremors. The big islands have thick forests, with ledges of rough grassland around the coast.

The people are Melanesians, like the people of New Guinea and the Solomon Islands. At first they lived by growing crops such as coconuts and by keeping pigs.

The first Europeans to visit were Portuguese explorers in 1606. In 1768 the French explorer Louis de Bougainville arrived. In 1774 the British explorer James Cook mapped the islands. He called them the New Hebrides, naming them after the Scottish Hebrides Islands.

From then on, France and Britain competed for any profit to be made out of the New Hebrides. Their interest led others to the islands. In many ways, it was the beginning of a bad time.

Dealers in sandalwood bribed the Melanesians with weapons. The tribes fought each other anyway, but the weapons made their wars even bloodier.

Australian planters sent ships to collect Melanesian labor for sugar plantations. Sometimes this was properly done: workers were hired and went only if they wanted to. But ships' captains were not always honest, and many Melanesians were tricked or kidnapped. Matters were made worse when pirates made the islands their base, and convicts escaped there from Australia.

Europeans, mainly French, began to lease land from local chiefs and cleared parts of the forest to make plantations. First they grew cotton. There was civil war in the United States, and US cotton was not for sale, so the cotton planters of the New Hebrides did well. When the US cotton trade revived after the war, New Hebrides planters had to find something else to grow. For a time it was coffee or bananas, but by about 1880 they found that coconuts made more profit.

The population began to change. The French planters brought in workers from French territories overseas. Some were Polynesians from the south Pacific. Many were from French colonies in southeast Asia. British planters began to worry about becoming a minority. They wanted their own government to take more interest in the islands.

In 1906 Britain and France agreed to control the New Hebrides jointly in an arrangement called a condominium. It did not work. There were two entirely separate governments, one for French colonists and one for British. They acted together on some things but separately on others. Native New Hebrideans were neglected by both. Christian missionaries set up some schools and clinics, but did not have enough money to do more.

During World War II there was no Japanese invasion as there was in the Solomon Islands, but the New Hebrides became an important military station, and the United States built the modern port of Santo as an air and naval base. Now Santo ships most of Vanuatu's coconut products.

After World War II the people found it hard to settle down again with the condominium. For years people argued over how to end it. In 1980 the New Hebrides became independent as the Republic of Vanuatu. Because English and French people still live there, English and French have been kept as two of the official languages. The other is Bislama. Numerous Melanesian languages are spoken as well. (See map on page 30.)

PITCAIRN

Few people live in Pitcairn, an isolated place in the southeastern Pacific Ocean. The main island was settled in 1790 by British sailors and other settlers from Tahiti. The sailors were mutineers from HMS *Bounty*, a British warship. They stayed in Pitcairn until 1856, when most of them moved away to Norfolk Island. The group includes three uninhabited islands: Henderson, Ducie, and Oeno. Pitcairn Island became a British colony in 1898; the others were added in 1902, and Pitcairn is ruled by Britain today. (See map on page 30.)

Lonely Pitcairn Island — sketched in 1873 — is the land farthest from any of the great continents.

NIUE

Niue is an island lying in the southern Pacific Ocean, south of Samoa and near the group called the Cook Islands. Niue was once part of the Cook Islands. With them, it was taken over by New Zealand in 1901. Ever since 1903 it has been governed separately, and today it is a self-governing territory of New Zealand. Its 5,000 people are Polynesian. (See map on page 30.)

NORFOLK ISLAND

Norfolk Island lies in the southwest Pacific Ocean, east of Australia and northwest of New Zealand. It was first settled by the families of mutineers from HMS *Bounty*, a British warship. They moved there from Pitcairn Island in 1856. It was once part of the Australian colony of New South Wales, but it has been self-governing since 1856 and is now a territory of Australia. (See map on page 30.)

NORTHERN MARIANAS

The Northern Mariana Islands are in the western Pacific Ocean, south of Japan. About 15,000 people of Micronesian stock live there. The islands were conquered by Spain in 1564 and were once held by Japan. After 1946 the United States governed them. In 1978 they became the Commonwealth of the Northern Marianas, in union with the United States. The Northern Marianas Islands are a large group. Their most important islands are Saipan and Tinian. (See map on page 30.)

PAPUA NEW GUINEA

The independent state of Papua New Guinea comprises the eastern part of the big island of New Guinea, which lies north of Australia, and also a group of little islands that includes New Britain and New Ireland.

About three million people, most of them Melanesians, live in Papua New Guinea. The original inhabitants came from southeast Asia to the island of New Guinea, which could be reached without long, dangerous sea voyages. As a result, New Guinea has attracted many different peoples at different times.

New Guinea is a huge island with a rugged jungle interior and big forests. The tribes could spread out and settle down quite separately from one another, so they developed many different customs and languages. But they had a similarity of appearance that, in the sixteenth century, led visiting Malay traders to call them Papuwa or Papuan ("frizzy-haired").

It is likely that the people have always lived as they do now. Their main activity is growing food. The tribes are led by chiefs, who have their bands of fighting men. But

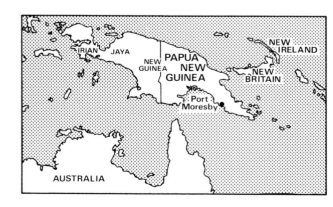

we know little of the Papuans' history. After the first ships visited New Guinea from abroad, it was a long time before foreign visitors explored inland.

Europeans trading in the area admired the Polynesian people. They thought them artistic and interesting. The Europeans' view of the Papuans was quite different, however. They found people with a Stone Age way of life and warriors masked with paint and mud. They decided to leave them alone. Perhaps this is why the Papuans survive in large numbers, with their customs unchanged.

Merchants from Germany were the first Europeans who really tried to explore New Guinea. They bought land and began plantations. In 1884 the north became a German colony.

The Germans left the local chiefs to manage their own people. There was really nothing else they could do. The Germans were anxious to learn everything about their new colony, but they could not get far enough inland to learn very much. The going was too hard and the tropical climate far too hot and sticky. Even after thirty years of rule, the Germans had very little idea how many Papuans there were.

In 1901 Australia began looking after the south. In 1921 its control also spread north because the Germans had been driven out during World War I (1914-18). The country became independent of Australia in 1975. White settlers remain. Most of them work in timber and mineral industries.

It was always difficult for outsiders to talk to the Papuans. After all, the many tribes have about 700 languages among them! Over the years, however, a form of English called pidgin English has evolved, and this has helped the varied peoples communicate with one another.

Mountainous jungles make transportation extremely difficult and isolate the interior from the outside world. Below, a helicopter lands supplies.

RÉUNION

The island of Réunion is in the Indian Ocean, east of Madagascar. Some of the smaller islands in this region are claimed jointly by Réunion, Madagascar, Mauritius, and the Seychelles. Réunion became a French colony in 1638. At that time the French called it Bourbon. Except for British occupation from 1810-14, the island has remained French. Today Réunion is an overseas department, or state, of France, just as Hawaii is a state of the United States. Its inhabitants are primarily of mixed African, Asian, and French origin. (See map on this page.)

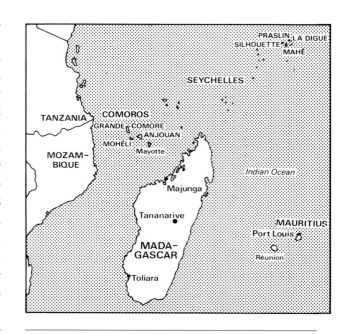

MAYOTTE

Mayotte is a small island in the Indian Ocean northwest of Madagascar. It became a French colony in 1843 and was ruled as one of the Comoros Islands until 1974, when the other Comoros became independent. But the people of Mayotte did not wish to cut their ties with France, so Mayotte remains a part of France today. The people are mostly of Malagasy, East African, and Arab descent. (See map on this page.)

MACAO

Macao, which is governed by Portugal, is on the coast of China at the mouth of the Canton River opposite Hong Kong. Macao consists of a peninsula linked to two islands by causeways. Its capital, Macao City, is on the peninsula. Macao became a Portuguese colony in 1557. In 1974 it became a territory of China administered by Portugal.

MADAGASCAR

Madagascar is a large island in the Indian Ocean. It lies opposite Mozambique, which is on the east coast of Africa.

Madagascar is approximately 1,000 miles (1,600 km) long, and 350 miles (560 km) across. A long, sandy coast faces the Indian Ocean, while inland, the ground rises steeply to the hilly countryside.

The first people probably arrived between AD 300 and 500. They came from what is now Indonesia, but their migration was a long, slow process.

At first, Indonesians left home to find trade routes to India. Gradually they went further around the shores of the Indian Ocean, settled at places on the east coast of Africa, and married into local families. These places became trading bases for Indonesia. Their people became a mixture of African and Indonesian.

About AD 300 the first of the traders came

to Madagascar. They settled in the north and west, on the coast. After AD 500 the number of traders coming to Madagascar increased. Africans were slowly crowding them out of the continent, and Arab ships were taking away much of their trade. The Afro-Indonesians moved on to Madagascar with its miles of empty land. There they began to settle as farmers and artisans.

They all had a common language, the same customs, and the same beliefs. Different groups developed as tribes, with different ways of life. Cattle herders lived on the western plains; crop growers lived on fertile land in the east; settlers who moved inland burned out forest clearings and planted rice.

When new settlers came, they usually lived on the coast. The most important new groups were East Africans and Arabs.

About AD 900 the first Arab trading towns appeared. The traders were not merchants straight from Arabia. They were people who had been slowly working their way down the east coast of Africa, like the Indonesians before them. They were a mixture of Arab, African, and Malagasy, which is what the people of Madagascar were called. Although they did not try to convert the Malagasy to the religion of Islam, their descendants sometimes won power over local people because they knew the sciences and medicine of Arabia. The Malagasy saw this knowledge as magic.

African settlers came to the west coast, probably from Mozambique. They introduced African farming methods, especially

The French were the first European colonists of Madagascar. Here, Malagasy chiefs are pledging their allegiance to the French governor in 1652.

Malagasy princesses encouraging their people to engage in a holy war against the country's French masters in the nineteenth century.

Suez Canal running through Egypt to link the Red Sea with the Mediterranean. European ships had to sail around the southern tip of Africa to get into the Indian Ocean. Madagascar was on this route and was therefore useful to both Britain and France as a source of supplies. Each country wanted to keep the other out.

The French had colonies in India and farther east. They had set up a town on Madagascar's east coast in 1643 and had stayed on the island ever since. From there they colonized Mauritius and Réunion.

But the French lost Mauritius and Réunion to Britain in 1810. Britain also had land in India and valuable trade with the east. They wanted to prevent the French from taking control of any point on the all-important shipping route.

So the British worked with Radama I to make his kingdom powerful enough to repel the French. British missionaries brought Christianity. British workers taught skills. But when Radama died, his widow turned against the British. And when in 1869 the Suez Canal was opened, Britain no longer needed to protect the southern route and lost interest in Madagascar.

The French did not lose interest, however. Helped by the Sakalava and Bara peoples, the French attacked the Merina kingdom in 1894-95. They and their allies won the war. Madagascar was united as a French protectorate.

In many ways the Malagasy people admired the French way of life and many wanted to make their country part of France,

in raising cattle. The Sakalava people of the west coast were mainly African. So were the Bara people of the southern inland areas. Both set up kingdoms that became strong in time.

It was the Merina kingdom, however, that would become the strongest. The Merina people, who were mainly Indonesian, lived in the hills of central Madagascar. Their first great king was Nampoina (1787-1810). He and his son Radama I conquered most of Madagascar by the time Radama died in 1828. Only pieces of the Sakalava and Bara kingdoms remained free.

Britain and France were then rivals in the Indian Ocean. At the time there was no with French citizenship for the people. But over time, they decided to work for independence instead.

In 1960 Madagascar became independent again, as it had been after the French conquest. But this time the country was a republic and not a kingdom as before.

PHILIPPINES

This country is actually a huge group of islands between the South China Sea and the Pacific Ocean. The two largest islands are Luzon and Mindanao, and another fourteen are big enough to be considered major islands. Altogether there are over seevn thousand islands and islets.

The early Filipino people lived by hunting and fishing and clearing small plots in their forests for crops. They lived in tribes, each with a chief. Most of the tribes kept on the move, going where the food was best. Only in the north did people settle in a particular place. There, on the hillsides of Luzon Island, they made terraces of earth on which to grow rice.

Like all island people, they learned how to travel by sea. They were trading with ports in southern China by AD 1000.

The Filipinos were animist in religion. This means they worshipped spirits that they believed to be in nature. After about 1400, traders brought the Muslim religion, Islam, to the southern island of Mindanao. By about 1550 there were two small Muslim states in the southern Philippines, and some of the Filipino chiefs were converted.

By that time the Spaniards were exploring the Pacific. They settled on one of the Philippine islands in 1565, conquered the country, and began to build a capital city at Manila. The Spaniards were not just looking for trade; they were anxious to spread the Roman Catholic religion. They did not convert the Muslims of the south, but Roman Catholic friars were sent to other areas as missionaries.

The Spaniards had already settled in Mexico. Their ships brought silver from Mexican mines and traded it for silks and other precious goods from China. Manila became the center of this trade.

In the countryside the friars settled their converts in villages built around new Catholic churches. With the help of the friars, the people in time became farmers instead of hunters. The friars also organized village governments and schools.

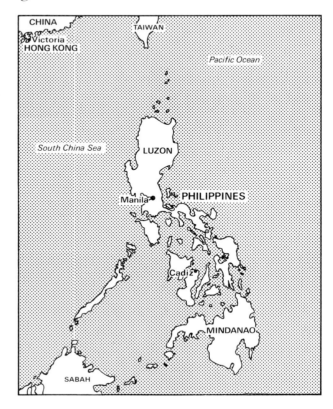

In 1830 Manila was opened to general trade because the Spanish trade link with Mexico had come to an end with the Mexican War of Independence. Now merchants could sell Philippine crops for export to any number of countries. The small village farms were replaced by big coffee and sugar plantations. Plantation owners became rich and sent their sons to be educated in Europe. These richer, better-educated people wanted more say in the government of their country, and by the late nineteenth century groups of Filipinos were taking hostile action against their Spanish rulers.

In 1898 Spain was at war with the United States. The US troops drove the Spaniards out of the Philippines. The Filipinos wanted independence, but by 1901 they had accepted US rule. It was always understood that they would be independent one day. That day came in 1946.

There are now about fifty-two million people in the Philippines. Many of them still speak American English and some speak Spanish. Of the many native languages in the Philippines, nine are widely spoken.

Ancient rice terraces cover the hillsides around this isolated village. However, the jungle waits for the first opportunity to close in again.

CHRISTMAS ISLAND

Christmas Island is a phosphate island, like Banaba, in Kiribati, and Nauru. It is in the Indian Ocean, south of Java, an island in Indonesia. Christmas Island became British in 1888. From 1900 until 1958 it was run by the British from Singapore, then one of Britain's possessions in Malaya. During World War II the Japanese occupied the island. In 1958 it was turned over to Australia, which administers the island as an external territory. It is populated mainly by Chinese and Malays. (See map on page 32.)

COCOS or KEELING ISLANDS

These islands lie in the Indian Ocean, about halfway between western Australia and Sri Lanka. The main islands are West Island, Home, Direction, South, Horsburgh and North Keeling islands. The first European to explore the islands was William Keeling in 1609. From 1886 to 1978, they belonged to the Clunies-Ross family, which had run coconut plantations there since about 1830. While the family owned the islands they shared the ruling of them with Britain until 1955. After 1955 the islands came under Australian rule, and in 1984 the islanders voted to become a part of Australia. The people are descended from imported workers — mainly Malays, other Asians, and a few East Africans. (See map on page 32.)

THE SOLOMON ISLANDS

The Solomon Islands are in the southwest Pacific Ocean, near New Guinea. This group consists of two parallel lines of high islands, with low islands scattered around them. The main islands, all mountainous, are Guadalcanal, Malaita, San Cristóbal, Santa Isabel, New Georgia, and Choiseul. The low islands include the Santa Cruz group, Ontong Java, and Rennell.

The people of the Solomons arrived at different times from two directions. The big, high islands were first settled by Melanesian people, who are probably among the earliest settlers in this part of the Pacific. They migrated from southeast Asia, through New Guinea.

The low islands, like the Santa Cruz group, are inhabited by Polynesian people. They came later, from the big islands of Polynesia to the east.

The climate of the main islands is hot, sticky, and wet. The landscape is characterized by thick, tropical rain forest. Fever is common. Most of the Melanesians lived in villages near the coast, but some tribes lived in the wet, forested valleys inland. They had many different languages, and many tribes could not understand each other.

Europeans have come to the Solomons as missionaries or planters. Few have been able to bear the climate for very long. Much of the land has belonged to Europeans, but the people have always been mainly Melanesian. In 1568 a Spaniard called Mendaña de Neyra found and named the islands. He came back in 1595, wanting to start a Spanish colony on Guadalcanal. But he could not find the islands he had seen in

1568, and he settled on the Santa Cruz group instead. The Spaniards tried to live there, but they left after Mendaña died. Few Europeans showed much interest in the Solomons for quite some time, and it would be the late nineteenth century before any European nations showed any interest in controlling parts of the island group again.

During the nineteenth century the Australians had established plantations in Queensland. They needed workers, so ships were sent to the Solomon Islands to get them. Some of the islanders were hired and went of their own accord, but others were tricked or bullied onto the ships by ship captains and carried off. Coastal villages lost many people. Solomon Islanders had never trusted or welcomed white men. This treatment by white men made them even more hostile.

By that time European interest in Pacific islands had grown. The northern Solomon Islands became a German protectorate in 1885, and the southern Solomons became a British protectorate in 1893.

German and British planters began to grow coconuts as a cash crop. In a short amount of time, the islands came to depend economically on the sale of copra, which is dried coconut meat. The Germans and British employed the islanders, who no longer went to work in Queensland. Most of the islanders actually lived on Malaita Island. But the plantations were on Guadalcanal, on Santa Isabel, and on smaller islands. The workers lived in camps on these islands.

During World War II (1939-45), the Japanese invaded the Solomon Islands. They were driven out after a time, but only after a terrible battle on Guadalcanal and some of the small islands.

After the war the coconut plantations were in ruins. The owners replanted where they could. But the people had changed, and many of them wanted a better life than plantation labor. They also wanted to be free of foreign control. A new capital was built at Honiara, which had been an airfield during the war.

In 1978 the Solomon Islands became an independent country. English is the official language, but many native languages are also spoken. (See map on page 30.)

The style of these canoes at Gizo Island has hardly changed since they brought the first settlers from Asia to the Solomons hundreds of years ago.

CAROLINES

The Caroline Islands are in the western Pacific Ocean, north of Papua New Guinea. These islands were colonized by Spain in the nineteenth century, sold to Germany in 1899, and governed by Japan after 1919 following Germany's defeat in World War I. Since 1947 they have been governed by the United States as part of the United States Trust Territory of the Pacific Islands. The main Caroline Islands are Truk, Yap, Palau, Kosrae, and Ponape. Palau is known as the Republic of Palau, and the others are known as the Federated States of Micronesia. The islands have a Micronesian population of about 60,000. (See map on page 30.)

FRENCH POLYNESIA

This is an area of the south Pacific Ocean where the islands are all dependencies of France. The largest group, called the Society Islands, includes Tahiti, Moorea, Raiatea, Huahine, Tahaa, Bora-Bora, and smaller islands. Tahiti is the best known of this group, and people on all the Society Islands speak Tahitian, which is a Polynesian language. East of the Society Islands are the Tuamotu Islands and Gambier Islands. North of the Tuamotus are the Marquesas Islands. South of the Society Islands are the Austral Islands, also called Tubuai.

All these came under French rule during the nineteenth century. They were protected by France from 1843 and ruled as French settlements after 1880. In 1958 they chose to become an overseas territory of France. (See map on page 30.)

AMERICAN SAMOA

The islands of eastern Samoa were put under the control of the United States after 1899 and became known as American Samoa. They are now a US territory. The islands of American Samoa are Tutuila, Aunu'u, Ta'u, Olosega, Ofu, and Rose. Swain's Island, which lies to the northwest, is also governed as part of eastern Samoa. For the history of all the Samoan islands and a map, see Western Samoa (page 10).

An 1876 sketch of a tamarind tree, supposed to have been planted on Venus Point, Tahiti, by Captain Cook.

TONGA

Tonga is a kingdom of about 170 islands in the southwest Pacific Ocean. The islands are scattered over 290 square miles (750 sq km), and most of them are very small. The western islands are volcanic and fertile; the eastern islands are made of coral. Three islands have always been important: Tongatapu in the south, Vava'u in the north, and Ha'apai in the middle.

The Tongans are Polynesian, like many people of the southern Pacific. They probably came to Tonga in about AD 300, moving east from Asia by canoe.

At first the Tongans lived under warlords. Even today many Tongans are tall, strong, and heavily built, and in ancient Tongan societies, warriors were among the most respected people. Rivalries between the fighting men of different war bands were not at all unusual.

In about AD 950 one of the warlords became king of all Tonga. He and his successors said that they were descended from the god called Tangaroa. This belief gave them a much greater hold over the people, for if the king was sacred as well as powerful, no enemy would dare to attack him. The kings were thus able to hold Tonga together and prevent rebellions among the warlords.

Under this sacred king developed a complicated society with many different classes. Class was also a key element of the Tongans' religion. Tongans believed that

Tongans put aside their modern clothes for a day, to dance in celebration of an ancient festival.

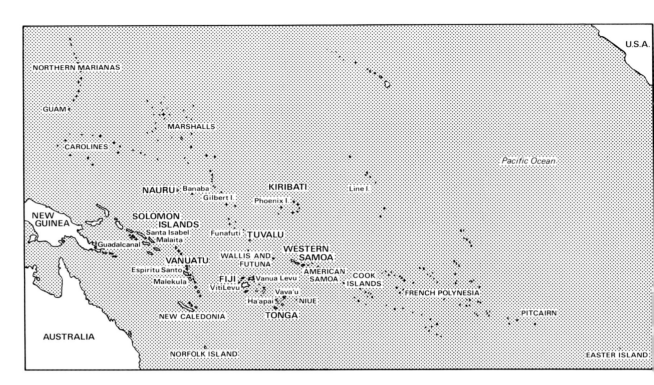

nobles went to a paradise when they died, but the common people did not.

Tongan rules were strict and discipline was sternly kept. All of this firm control over their beliefs and behavior brought peace and gave Tongans a chance to concentrate on farming and building. The people lived not in villages but on their own plantations, where they terraced fertile land with stone walls. Tonga became powerful among neighboring states. With no wars at home, Tongan warriors went off to fight elsewhere.

All this order and stability in Tongan life depended on the power of the ruler. By 1770 this power had weakened. The warlords became powerful again, especially in the north. In 1799 the head of the government was murdered, and civil war broke out. Many Tongans fled to Fiji, which lies to the west. The old form of government came to an end.

In 1820 a new ruler, George Tupou, came into power. He ended the wars and by 1845 had reunited Tonga. King George was a member of the Wesleyan church, so he encouraged his people to convert to Christianity. This presented his people with a problem. Under the old religion, the gods were said to protect the king and give him some of their own strength. The people felt that King George had cut himself off from this strength by becoming a Christian. This took away much of his authority over them. So any new government that King George might set up with the help of Christian missionaries would have to be perfect to make up for his loss of sacred power.

The Wesleyan church produced a leader, but he was far from perfect. This leader managed to take control of every government post as well as of the church, but he managed things so badly that in 1890 he was forced to depart. This left no government at all. The king was afraid that new warlords would start another civil war. So the British, who ruled nearby Fiji at that time, agreed to send a Prime Minister, and in 1900 Britain and Tonga had signed a treaty for the protection of Tonga by Britain.

This treaty remained in force until Tonga became independent in 1970.

The Wesleyan church recovered, and today most Tongans belong to it. There are now about ninety-nine thousand of them, and their current king is a descendant of George Tupou.

This massive trilithon — a three-stoned arch — is evidence of a settlement centuries ago on the Tonganese islands.

INDONESIA

Indonesia consists of a long arc of islands, stretching for about 3,200 miles (about 5,120 km). The big islands are Sumatra, Java, and Sulawesi. Most of the big island of Borneo as well as the western part of New Guinea island are also part of Indonesia. The small islands include Timor and Bali. All the islands together form the Republic of Indonesia.

Most of what we know about early Indonesia comes from Java and Sumatra. For example, we know that the people grew rice on the fertile soil along the rivers and near the coast and that villages joined forces to organize work. One project that demanded many workers and an overall plan was making channels to take water through fields. We also know that a local chief ruled groups of villages. Groups that built ships took up trading by sea. After AD 400 people often sailed to China.

China's trade with countries farther west moved down through the South China Sea and up through the Strait of Malacca, which serves as a passage between Malaya and Sumatra. Palembang, in Sumatra, became the greatest Indonesian port for this trade. The rulers of Palembang became powerful, and their kingdom, called Srivijaya, controlled the Strait. Ideas as well as trade traveled through the Strait. Merchants and missionaries came from India, bringing the Hindu religion. Buddhist priests came too. By the year AD 700 Palembang was both a rich port and a capital city, and a center of religious teaching.

Indonesians altered the Indian religions by adding ideas of their own. This mixed religion spread to Java and many of the other islands. The kings of central Java built great Buddhist temples and monuments. The kings themselves were considered gods.

Srivijaya remained the greatest kingdom until about 1200. After that arose the powerful rule of princes in east Java. Another sort of power came along the trade routes from India as Indian merchants of the Muslim faith began to set up small trading centers along the coasts of Indonesia. By 1300 several centers had become states. Wars broke out, particularly between the kings of the Mataram kingdom in Java and the Muslim states on Java's north coast. The Mataram kings destroyed these states, ending

their hold on trade throughout the area.

In the seventeenth century, Europeans wanted to trade in Indonesia. They particularly desired the spices that grew in eastern Indonesia and sold for high prices in Europe. The Dutch competed with Britain and Portugal to make trading agreements with local rulers throughout Indonesia.

In 1619 Dutch merchants founded Batavia — now Djakarta, the capital of Indonesia — as the center of their trading empire. As time passed, merchants could not help becoming involved in the affairs of the Mataram kingdom. Mataram kings gave Dutch merchants land in return for their help. The

Above, an old but serviceable steam engine pulls a load of sugar cane from the fields to the factory.

The coffee harvest. The seeds from these berries will be dried, roasted, and ground into coffee.

power of the kings among their people was becoming weaker. By 1755 Dutch merchants held most of Java and were taking on problems that only a government could tackle. Trade began to decline. By 1799 the company had collapsed. During the nineteenth century the Dutch government ruled Java, and eventually, the rest of Indonesia as well.

Governing such a large place was expensive. The Dutch came up with two ways to produce the necessary money. First, villages had to set aside land for export crops. Second, Europeans were allowed to lease land and set up large plantations, growing more export crops and employing local labor.

Both changes made money for the Europeans, but also caused resentment. Nationalist movements began after 1900. By 1927 Achmed Sukarno began working for independence.

During World War II (1939-45) the Japanese occupied Indonesia. This hastened the end of Dutch rule. In 1945 Sukarno declared the country independent. After much fighting, the Dutch agreed in 1949 to Indonesian independence.

Modern Indonesia has about 158 million people. Strife among the many regions and nationalities within Indonesia persists to this day. To help unify the people, the government has replaced the Dutch language with the Indonesian language.

Australian scientists and crew members of an ice ship haul in freshly killed seals to feed their huskies. These dogs provide transportation in the snowy wastes.

ANTARCTICA

Antarctica, at the South Pole, is the world's fifth largest continent and by far the coldest. The lowest temperature ever recorded on Earth, -126.9°F (-88.3°C), was in Antarctica on August 24, 1960. Including the ice shelves around its edge, Antarctica's area covers around 5.5 million square miles (14 million sq km). Even the mainland is mostly made of ice. In fact, scientists think that 90% of the world's ice is in Antarctica! There are no countries or towns in Antarctica because the climate is too cold. But scientists and explorers have made bases there, and seven countries — Norway, Australia, France, New Zealand, Britain, Chile, and Argentina — have claimed territory.

Other countries, including the United States and the Soviet Union, do not recognize these claims, and no further claims have been allowed since the Antarctic Treaty of 1961.

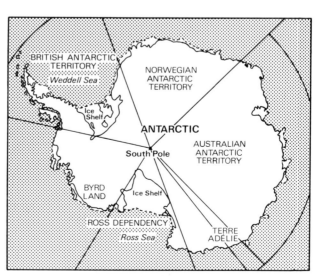

NEW CALEDONIA

New Caledonia is made up of a big island and a scattering of smaller ones. These include the Loyalty Islands, the Isle of Pines and the Belep Islands. The islands lie in the southwest Pacific Ocean, east of Australia and northwest of New Zealand. New Caledonia became a French dependency in 1853 and is now an overseas territory of France. The people are Melanesian. (See map on page 30.)

MARSHALLS

The Marshalls lie east of the Caroline Islands in the western Pacific. About 25,000 people of Micronesian stock live there. The islands were held by Germany in the nineteenth century, and after 1919, following Germany's defeat in World War I, they were governed by Japan. Since 1947 they have been governed by the United States as part of the United States Trust Territory of the Pacific Islands. The chief Marshall Islands are Majuro, Kwajalein, and Jaluit. (See map on page 30.)

FIJI

Fiji is a country made up of about 330 islands. About 110 are inhabited.

The islands cover a big area in the south Pacific Ocean — about 7,078 square miles (18,333 sq km). The large islands are Viti Levu and Vanua Levu.

Fiji is the farthest east of the islands called Melanesia. *Melanesia* means "black

islands," the name invented by the first European travelers who found people with very dark skin and black hair living on these islands. Melanesia also includes the islands of New Guinea, the Solomons, Vanuatu, and New Caledonia.

Fijians resemble the other people of Melanesia in their tall, dark, and muscular appearance, but they are like the people of Polynesia (the southeastern Pacific) in the way they live.

Early Fijians who came eastward by canoe settled in Fiji by about AD 300. They were quite good at almost everything they attempted. Fijian tools, weapons, pottery, canoes, and buildings were greatly admired, and even their neighbors, the Tongans, who were clever themselves, often asked their advice.

Fijians also had a reputation as fierce warriors. This reputation kept them safe from invasion, but it certainly didn't stop the many fights that broke out among Fijian chiefs and warriors.

In the late eighteenth century Chief Nailatikau, from the small Fijian island of Bau, began a civil war. He was helped by Tongan warriors who had settled in Fiji earlier. The war was made worse when Europeans — most of them traders — came to Fiji and joined in. These traders bought and sold Fijian sandalwood from 1804 until 1813, when supplies ran out. During that time the traders bribed Fijian suppliers with guns and gave sailors weapons to help them fight their enemies. Fijians themselves

A young crop of sugar cane. The need for workers in the sugar plantations caused the immigration of Indian laborers in the late nineteenth century.

captured ships and used the heavy guns to blow up enemy villages.

Through these wars, the chiefs of Bau became the strongest, and the Bau chief Cakobau became King of Fiji in 1852.

Cakobau could not control all of Fiji, so he looked elsewhere for help. By that time the Tongans were a powerful group in Fiji, with a Christian king who was anxious to spread Christianity in Fiji as well. Cakobau won Tonga's help by announcing that he, too, had become a Christian. It soon became clear, however, that Tonga wanted to take control of Fiji.

Around the same time, another powerful group of people began to make its presence felt in Fiji — white settlers. Because of the civil war in the United States, supplies of American cotton had dried up and dealers looked for places where they could grow it themselves. By 1868 about 2,500 settlers, most of them from Australia, had begun to plant cotton in Fiji.

Cakobau could not control either the white settlers or the Tongans. In 1867 the islands were divided into two groups. Cakobau ruled one group, the one with the white settlers, and Tonga ruled the other.

In 1874 the whole of Fiji was offered to Britain and reunited as a British colony.

The Fijians had endured much hardship. After suffering years of civil war, nearly a third of them were killed by an epidemic in the 1870s. The British were afraid that the Fijians would die out as a nation and, more important to the British, as a source of labor. When the settlers started their sugar plantations, they needed hundreds of laborers to work on them. Thinking Fijian workers would no longer be

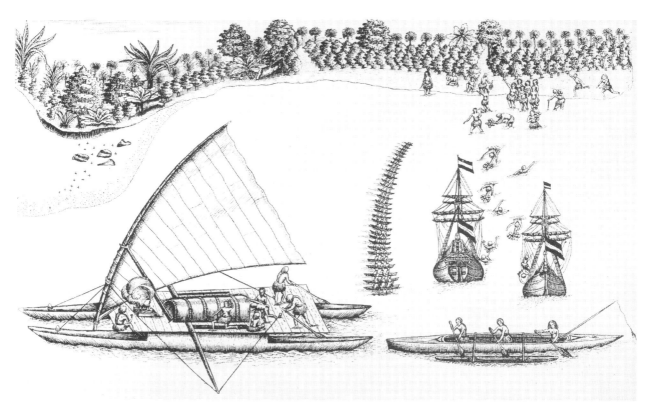

available locally, the settlers brought in workers from India.

The Fijians, however, were not dying out, and the two groups — native Fijians and Indians — have since had to figure out how to live with each other.

In 1970 Fiji became an independent country again. Its population now numbers about 700 thousand people, and Christianity is widespread, as is Hinduism, for more than half the people are of Indian descent. (See map on page 30.)

KIRIBATI

Kiribati is a new country. It is made up of several groups of islands and stretches across thousands of miles of the Pacific Ocean. But the total land area is only some 264 square miles (684 sq km). Beginning at the island of Banaba in the west, the outline of Kiribati has the shape of a tropical fish. The "body" swells out around the Gilbert Islands, narrows at the Phoenix Islands, and flares out into the ocean in the broad "tail" of the Line Islands.

Three of the Line Islands do not belong to Kiribati. Kingman Reef, Jarvis, and Palmyra belong to the United States, but nobody lives there. In fact, only three of the Line Islands are inhabited. One is Teraina (once called Washington); the other two inhabited islands are Tabuaeran (Fanning) and Kiritimati (Christmas Island). These two islands have coconut plantations run by people from the Gilbert Islands.

The Phoenix Islands are uninhabited; the Gilbert Islands have about 52 thousand people, many of whom live on Tarawa.

The people are Micronesian, a word that means "from the place of small islands." They probably came at first from eastern Asia but developed their own language and their own way of life in the Gilberts. These low, coral islands produce little. The coral rock and sandy soil are not fertile, and the flat land does not attract rain. So the people of the low islands have learned to travel to neighboring places to buy what they need. Even today, Gilbert Islanders are famous for their sailing ability. They use the same sort of navigation as the Polynesians, but their canoes are different and quite fast.

On land, their main concern was to get and defend enough ground to grow food. Because so little fertile land was available, the people developed complicated systems for keeping land in groups of families.

There are sixteen Gilbert Islands. Eleven have lagoons — calm water sheltered by a reef on one side of the island. The other side is open to the ocean. Fishing villages lie along the lagoon shore, and the wild side of each island has often been the place of worship. Before British missionaries arrived, Gilbert Islanders, like their fellow Micronesians elsewhere, believed in many gods and spirits and in the power of their tribal ancestors.

About AD 1300 people from Samoa invaded the Gilbert Islands and set up their own High Chiefs. This rule went on in the northern Gilbert Islands for centuries. But the idea of High Chiefs did not take hold in the south and the people returned to their old system of ruling through councils.

In the eighteenth century, the British began taking an active interest in the islands. British explorer Thomas Gilbert named the islands after himself following a visit in 1788; British missionaries arrived during the nineteenth century to teach Christianity to the local people; and the Gilbert Islands became a protectorate of Britain in 1892.

In 1900 the island of Banaba was included in the protectorate. Including Banaba proved to be an economically sound move by the British. Phosphate was produced on Banaba; the profits paid much of the cost of running the other islands.

In 1915 the protectorate became a colony. It now seemed sensible to the British that the nearest island neighbors, the Ellice Islands, now Tuvalu, be brought into the colony, despite one problem: the Ellice Islanders are Polynesian and speak a different language.

The British had problems with Banaba, too. Phosphate had become a major source of income for just about everyone except the Banabans, who felt their island was being destroyed by the mining. By 1945 the Banabans had gotten enough of the profits to buy themselves another island.

The argument about the phosphate income went on until 1979, the year Banaba and the Gilbert, Phoenix, and Line islands became independent as the Republic of Kiribati. Tuvalu had become independent on its own in 1978. (See map on page 30.)

JAPAN

Japan is a nation that comprises a group of islands in the western Pacific Ocean, off the mainland of Asia. The main islands, from north to south, are Hokkaido, Honshu, Shikoku, and Kyushu. The Ryukiu and Bohin islands belong to Japan.

Japan has many steep mountains. This means that only about one-sixth of the land is fertile lowland that can be farmed. So competition for land has always been keen. In fact, the right to own land, or grow food on it, has been a major concern through most of Japan's history.

The earliest people in Japan lived by hunting and fishing, but by about AD 500 their descendants had moved down onto the fertile plains, where the land was better suited for growing food crops. Honshu island, especially the part between Kobe and Tokyo, was the first settled area. There the land was good for growing rice in paddy fields. Soon the people had grown food enough to support many small towns, while in northern Japan the people still lived as scattered tribes, hunting in the hills.

The Honshu people were grouped in families, or clans. All the clans looked up to the emperor. He was their overlord and their chief priest, but he did not always have much effective control over them.

The people had a simple religion. They worshipped the spirits of their ancestors and the gods of nature. In the sixth century, the Buddhist religion came to Japan from China, along with other Chinese ideas about government and art.

The Japanese were, and are, independent island people, cut off from the mainland of Asia. They could choose whether to bring in and to accept foreign ideas or not. And whenever they did bring foreign ideas, they usually changed them and adapted them to their own needs. Buddhism was affected by their old religion, which the people went on practicing and which they now call Shinto, "the way of the gods."

In AD 700 the emperor built the first capital city, at Nara. The emperors, who claimed to be descended from the Sun Goddess, now tried to be strong rulers with real power over the clans. But the clan leaders and their warriors, called *samurai*, were too strong to be controlled. Many

In Japan there is an ancient tradition of theater. This painting is of an actor in the costume of a samurai, or warrior.

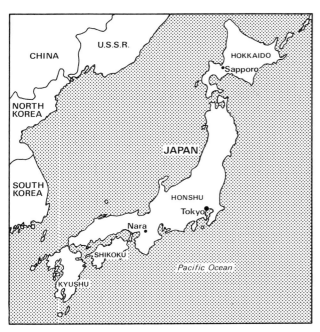

clans held mountainous land that was difficult to attack, where they did as they liked.

By 1192 conditions had become so bad that the emperor created a new kind of officer to keep the peace. This was the Shogun. The first Shogun set up his own fortress-city and soon found himself acting as a civil governor as well as the commander of troops.

In time the Shoguns became the real rulers of Japan, but it took them centuries to master the clans.

After 1550 European traders and Christian missionaries came to Japan. The clans, which were still warlike, hoped to buy foreign weapons they could use to fight each other or the government. They also hoped to use Christianity against the big Buddhist monasteries, which had become

A young woman in the traditional dress of a noble lady is celebrating the Aoi festival in Kyoto.

quite powerful. For these two reasons, the chiefs welcomed the foreigners.

In 1603 Tokugawa Ieyasu became Shogun. The Tokugawa family ruled until 1868. They brought all Japan under their control, banning everything the clan chiefs could use to make trouble. They banned Christianity in 1614, expelled foreign merchants in 1639, and forbade all contact with foreign states, with the exception of a small amount of foreign trade.

The country became peaceful. Many clan chiefs and samurai even became civil governors or businessmen. But people had to live by hundreds of strict rules.

By 1850 the Shoguns had become weak rulers and faced growing discontent from their people. Western countries wanted to resume trade and other contact. The way this was done — through a display of military force more than through good will — upset everybody. Civil discontent became civil war, and the Shoguns' rule ended in 1868. All of this tumult was accompanied by a great revival of loyalty to the emperor, who was still regarded as a god.

The emperor was made head of a new government. His ministers wanted to do two things: first, to make Japan so strong that foreign countries could not force her to do anything; and second, to make Japan a rich industrial country.

At first these two aims fitted together. Japanese armies conquered parts of the nearby Asian mainland and used the resources there for Japanese industry. But

A bull draws a cart decorated with wisteria, iris, and plum blossom during the Aoi Matsuri festival.

Japan's triumphs gave the nation a real taste for power and led to a period when the army had more say than anyone else about Japanese policy. The military's goal was to become a great Japanese empire, stretching through southeast Asia and the Pacific islands.

It was the pursuit of this ambition that took the Japanese into World War II in 1941. In 1945, after the United States devastated Hiroshima and Nagasaki with atomic bombs, Japan surrendered and the war was ended.

The United States, which had won the war against Japan, then occupied the country. The United States introduced the Japanese to many ideas about industry and government. The US occupation lasted until 1952. During the occupation, a new kind of government grew; the emperor was still head of state but no longer ruled and was no longer regarded as divine.

Modern Japan continued to improve upon the industries founded after 1868. Many Japanese products are now famous all over the world.

GUAM

Guam is the largest of the Mariana Islands and the farthest south. It lies in the western Pacific Ocean, south of Japan and east of the Philippines. In the sixteenth century the island was conquered by Spain, who lost it to the United States in 1898. Today Guam is a territory of the States, which uses the island as an important military base. There are more than 100 thousand people living there, but fewer than half are descended from the island's original Micronesian inhabitants. (See map on page 30.)

AUSTRALIA

Australia is both a country and a continent. The mainland is divided into five states and two territories, one of which, the Australian Capital Territory, includes the nation's capital city, Canberra. The sixth state is Tasmania, an island off the southeast coast.

Macquarie Island, far to the south, is part of Tasmania. Lord Howe Island to the east is part of the state of New South Wales.

The first Australians probably came from Indonesia at least 40 thousand years ago. They lived by hunting and by gathering wild food. They learned how to survive in

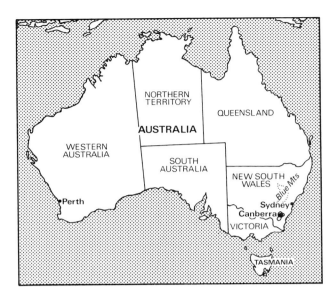

NORTHERN TERRITORY

QUEENSLAND

AUSTRALIA

WESTERN AUSTRALIA

SOUTH AUSTRALIA

NEW SOUTH WALES

Blue Mts

Perth

Sydney
Canberra

VICTORIA

TASMANIA

a very dry climate like that of central, northern, and western Australia. Their life was simple, but their beliefs and customs were — and still are — complex. The British, the first European settlers, called these people Aborigines. The British settlement was begun in 1788 in New South Wales, where Sydney is today. It started as a prison, to ease the overcrowded prisons of Britain. When the British discovered that the land was good for grazing sheep, soldiers and ex-convicts alike began to breed sheep and export wool.

By 1813 sheep farmers had crossed the Blue Mountains that lie inland. Beyond the Blue Mountains, sheep farmers spread north, south, and west, pleased that they found good pasture in all directions.

In those days, every detail in the lives of the European settlers seemed to depend on the grazing sheep. People argued about the right to own or use grassland and about who was going to do the work. Big landowners brought in workers from Asia

The giant coal dredger opposite is cutting soft, brown coal in an open-pit mine in Morwell, Victoria.

Below is a scene in a sheep-shearing shed. Sheep were brought from Europe to create Australia's first big industry.

and the Pacific islands who would work for less money than the British settlers and ex-convicts.

In 1851 gold was found at Bathurst, in New South Wales. When more gold was found in the new colony of Victoria and in Western Australia, a great rush of new immigrants swept the continent. These people needed work and food. To meet this need — and to cash in on it — a new kind of "rush" began. People developed new trades and industries, built railways, and established new towns. They bought precious metals. Soon farmers were raising not only sheep but cattle, wheat, and sugar cane.

By 1860 colonies had grown in Queensland, South Australia, Western Australia, Tasmania, Victoria, and New South Wales. Australia is so big and has so many kinds of land and climate that the separate colonies depended on different resources.

Each colony tried to protect its particular wealth. To add to the isolation, huge deserts in the center separated east and west. Europeans had explored these deserts in the 1830s but discovered they could not live there. As a result, isolated settlements were scattered around the coast.

In the late nineteenth century, European countries began to control nearby Pacific islands. Australians felt they would be safer if they were united, so in 1901, the Commonwealth of Australia replaced the old group of British colonies.

Australia's European population was still of British descent. Then World War II came to an end and left many people in Europe with nowhere to live. Australia needed people, so European immigrants were invited in. Thousands came from Italy, Greece, Poland, and other countries. After that the non-native population was no longer all English-speaking, but it was still all European. In 1974, however, Australia's immigration policy changed again. Asians could now settle in Australia.

There are now about fifteen million Australians. About 160 thousand of them are Aborigines, most of them living in the north and west.

Wheat was grown in Australia in the early nineteenth century. The photograph opposite, taken about 1850, shows horse teams pulling the plow.

In the picture above, members of the Korean community, who settled in Australia in the 1970s, join the celebrations for Australia's National Day.

Another early industry was grapes for wine. The lower picture shows dancing at the Barossa Valley wine festival in South Australia.

TUVALU

Tuvalu is a country in the central Pacific Ocean, north of Fiji. It is made up of nine islands, of which eight have villages. The main island is Funafuti.

The islands are narrow, low-lying, and flat. They stretch across the ocean 360 miles (580 km), but altogether they make up a land area of only ten square miles (26 sq km). About 7,500 people live there.

The first people to live there were Polynesians who came from Samoa about 300 years ago. They traveled by canoe, a journey of hundreds of miles. Polynesian canoes were able to cover long distances, so people from Samoa and nearby islands settled all over the central and east Pacific in this way. Their fleets of big canoes carried people, food, and livestock. They knew how to study the clouds, the stars, and the movement of the waves so as to stay on course. But although they had great knowledge, they had no power except that of wind and sail, so if they were blown off course there was nothing they could do about it. Many small islands, like Tuvalu, may have been found that way by accident.

Once found, the Tuvalu islands were not easy to live on. Much of Tuvalu is coral reef and coral atoll. The people who found Tuvalu had to learn how to manage on tiny strips of sand and coral, perched on top of a submarine mountain. Sometimes they were swamped by ocean storms. They had little rain, because flat islands have no hills to attract rain clouds.

Children wearing traditional grass skirts enjoy themselves during the annual Youth Day.

The people built fishing villages on the lagoon side of the islands. They did not go to the open, ocean side of their islands except to worship their gods and to call up spirits. They dug down in the dry soil until they reached a level where it was damp, and there they grew their food in pits. Their main resources were the coconut trees, which provide food, drink, cooking oil, timber, clothing, and rope.

At times when there was not enough food, they loaded the canoes again and moved on. The last of these moves was in 1948, when people from Tuvalu settled on Kioa, in Fiji.

White men first saw the islands in 1568. About 250 years later, in 1819, a British ship again came upon them. The captain called them the Ellice Islands, after a member of the British Parliament.

More British ships visited the islands, as did ships from Australia. These were collecting workers for the plantations in Australia and in other places where white settlers needed workers. Some Ellice Islanders went of their own accord, but others were bullied or deceived into going.

In 1892 the chiefs agreed that their islands should be protected and governed by Britain. From 1915 until 1975 the Ellice Islands were joined with the Gilbert Islands, now part of Kiribati, to make a British colony. But the customs of the two peoples are quite different, and they speak different languages. After a time the Ellice Islanders decided they would rather be on their own.

In 1978 Tuvalu became independent again, under its old name. (See map on page 30.)

THE MALDIVES

The Maldives are islands in the Indian Ocean, southwest of Sri Lanka. The Maldives are hundreds of islands, of which 219 are inhabited by about 160 thousand people of mainly Ceylonese and other Asian stock. The whole group makes up an independent republic.

The early people probably came from Sri Lanka. They were Buddhists, who arrived about AD 500. People in the Maldives still speak Devehi, a language similar to that of early Sri Lanka.

The people lived then, as they do now, by fishing and by growing food. The Maldives are low-lying coral islands that produce coconuts and fruit.

During the twelfth century, travelers from India and Sri Lanka brought a new religion to the Maldives. This was Islam, which is now the state religion. The Muslim rulers of the Maldives were sultans, but it was difficult for them to keep their small, scattered state independent. Hundreds of tiny, flat islands are nearly impossible to defend.

During the seventeenth century, therefore, the sultans put their islands under the protection of their nearest neighbor, Sri Lanka.

By 1887 Sri Lanka itself was ruled by the British, who then brought the Maldives under their control as well, although the sultans still reigned. This arrangement lasted until 1965, when the Maldives became independent.

In 1968 the rule of the sultans ended, and the country became a republic.

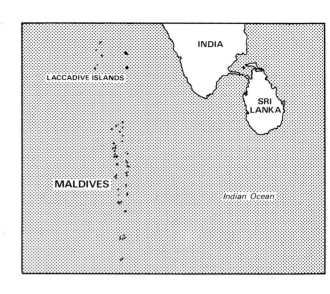

SINGAPORE

Singapore is a republic founded in 1965. The state lies on an island that is joined by causeway to the southern tip of Malaya. Singapore also comprises more than fifty little islands. About 2.5 million people live in Singapore, most of them of Chinese descent. The other major groups are Malays and Indians. Singapore is a busy port and commercial city.

For a map and the history of Singapore as a city-state in what is today Malaysia, see the discussion of Malaysia on pages 4-7.

THE COOK ISLANDS

The Cook Islands were named after the British explorer James Cook. Of the fourteen islands in the group, the most important is Rarotonga. The islands lie in the southern Pacific Ocean, northeast of New Zealand and southwest of Samoa. They became a British protectorate in 1883. In

1901 they were taken over by New Zealand, and they became a self-governing territory of New Zealand in 1965. About 20 thousand Polynesian people live there. (See map on page 30.)

One of the most famous Polynesian islands is Easter Island. The first European visitors were amazed to find an advanced civilization, with these giant statues, existing thousands of miles from any continent.

EASTER ISLAND

Easter Island is a Polynesian island that belongs to Chile. It lies in the eastern Pacific Ocean, isolated from other island groups. The island was named by a Dutch explorer who landed on it on Easter Day in 1722. It has belonged to Chile since 1888. Some people believe the original inhabitants of Easter Island may have traveled from South America over a thousand years ago and built huge statues called megaliths. They also believe Polynesian ancestors of the present inhabitants sailed in canoes to Easter Island, fought and killed the native inhabitants, and made the island their home for centuries to come. (See map on page 30.)

NEW ZEALAND
JOURNAL OF
Agriculture
JANUARY · 1949

NEW ZEALAND

New Zealand is a group of islands in the southern Pacific Ocean. North Island and South Island are the largest, but many smaller islands — such as Kermadec, to the north, and Tokelau, far to the northeast — are also part of New Zealand.

People from the Pacific Islands probably came to North Island after AD 1000. They fished and did simple farming. These people were Polynesians, a group still living in the eastern Pacific Islands.

During the fourteenth century, other Polynesians came. They called themselves Maori, which means "people who belong

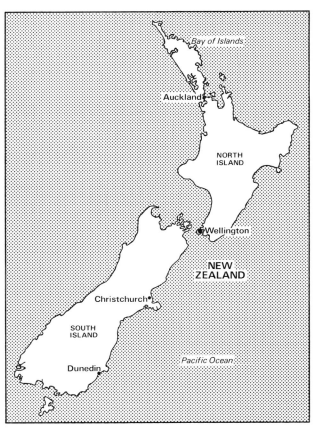

The painting opposite illustrates the signing of the Treaty of Waitangi in 1840. It marked the birth of the modern state, and is now commemorated as New Zealand's National Day.

The naval explorer Captain Cook was the first European to establish that New Zealand was a group of islands. The picture above shows his death on Tahiti.

here." They called the earlier settlers Moriori, which means "not as good as we are," and drove them out. The Moriori went down to South Island and the offshore islands and have since died out.

The Maoris lived in tribes. Their world was highly organized. Each tribe held its land and lived there according to the rules of religion and of the tribal chief. The group was much more important than the individual, because without the group and its land, the individual would die.

The Maoris were also quite warlike. The tribes never united. They often fought each other, as well as any Europeans who came near their coasts.

The first of these Europeans was an explorer who came from Holland in 1642. Europeans named the islands New Zealand because Zealand is the name of a place in Holland. No Europeans tried to make permanent colonies until 1814.

The first colony was at the Bay of Islands, in North Island. It was set up by missionaries who had come from New South Wales, in Australia, hoping to convert the Maoris to Christianity.

The Maoris held the fertile land and grew the food, so the missionaries had to buy from them whatever they needed. This they did, giving the Maoris guns and blankets in return for food. The guns made their tribal wars far more deadly, and the blankets became soaked in the wet weather and

Modern-day Maoris in traditional dress with a traditional wood carving.

Opposite, early settlers hunt for sperm whales from open boats off the rugged South Island coast.

made the wearers ill. The Maoris' society and way of life began to decline as the number of white settlers grew.

Nearly all the settlers were British or Australians of British stock. A British company called the New Zealand Company set up trading colonies, and Australians came to trade with the Maoris and to hunt whales off the coast. In 1840 Britain made a treaty with the Maoris by which it was agreed that New Zealand should be a British colony.

It didn't take long for arguments and misunderstandings to arise over land. The settlers, like most Europeans, were used to the idea of one person buying land with money and holding it as his or her own property. The owner would then hire workers and pay them in money for so many hours' work on the land. Both these ideas were foreign to the Maoris. Bitter arguments arose over land the settlers thought they had bought. In 1845 the arguments turned into a war that lasted until 1871.

During the war, gold was found in both of the main islands. This brought in more settlers and more money. Soon New Zealand had a bigger white population, rich

Wool is New Zealand's biggest industry. The country has twenty times as many sheep as people.

enough to build railways and ports and to farm big areas of land. During the war, the Maoris had become poorer and fewer. They knew they would have to survive by fitting in with the way of life that had replaced their own. This is what they have done.

New Zealand is now a farming country, raising sheep, cattle, and grain. The colony became independent in 1907. Today there are about three million New Zealanders, of whom about 300 thousand are Maoris. The North Island holds most of the population. The South Island, with its smaller, more rural population, has good grassland in the east, a large area of mountains — once volcanoes — and active geysers, fountains of hot water gushing out of the earth.

THE SEYCHELLES

The Seychelle Islands are in the Indian Ocean. They lie north of Madagascar and are divided into two groups. Their land area is only 171 square miles (444 sq km), but they spread out over 150,000 square miles (400,000 sq km).

The main group is the one farther from Madagascar. It has forty islands, of which Mahé, Praslin, La Digue, Silhouette, Frigate, and North Islands are inhabited. All these are granite mountain islands, thickly covered with tropical plants and trees. Mahé is the largest, 56 square miles (144 sq km). Most of the people live there.

The outer group, which lies toward Madagascar, contains sixty coral islands. They are small, flat, and widely scattered.

In 1609 a company of merchants from

Europe found the Seychelles uninhabited. They were impressed by the beautiful forests and by such rare wild creatures as the giant tortoise.

In 1756 the French took the islands. France at that time held Mauritius, to the south, and from there began to settle people on the Seychelles. Colonists came, bringing with them their East African slaves. They began to export the natural produce of the islands. By 1789, however, they had done so much damage to the forests and to wildlife that the French government stopped their trade. The settlers turned to farming. More people arrived, including many people deported from France.

In 1814 the Seychelles became British. Few British settlers came to the islands, so even though English was used in government, it was not widely spoken. The people were still the original mixture of African and French. Their language was French or Creole, a mixture of French and African dialects. Their religion was Roman Catholic.

During the 1830s the government abolished slavery, so the settlers turned to a new kind of farming that employed fewer workers. They set up plantations of trees and bushes that needed little attention, such as coconuts and cinnamon.

In 1836 a French botanist learned how to grow the vanilla vine away from its natural home, Mexico, so vanilla became still another valuable export crop for the Seychelles.

By 1900 the islands had some British, Indian, Chinese, and Malay people, all attracted by the plantations and their export trade. The majority were still of French, African, or mixed descent.

The islands became an independent republic in 1976. Today the main language is Creole; the other official languages are English and French. (See map on page 18.)

The abolition of slavery caused the settlers to look for a crop that required few paid workers. The perfect answer was coconuts.

BRUNEI

On the north coast of the island of Borneo lies Brunei, a small state ruled by a sultan.

Much of inland Borneo is thick forest, and the people live much as the early population lived — by hunting, fishing and farming in little patches of cleared forest. Borneo had many original tribes. The biggest of these were the Dyaks, the Ibans, and the Kadazan.

Around the coast, things were quite different from inland. During the Middle Ages many small ports were set up by foreign merchants — and pirates — who had ships in the South China Sea. Many of these places had been settled by people from Indonesia and Malaya. These people held the Muslim faith, Islam, which had reached them along sea-trade routes from India.

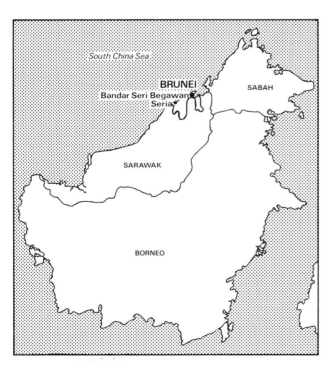

Brunei began in about AD 1500 as one of these small Muslim towns. At that time Malacca, in Malaya, was the main center for Muslim merchants in the far east. In 1511 Malacca was conquered by the Portuguese. The merchants then made Brunei into their new base. It became both rich and powerful — the strongest state in Borneo. By 1545, when the Portuguese wanted to ship their trade from Malacca to the islands east of Borneo, they had to get the Sultan's permission to sail around his coast.

While the southern part of the island became part of what is now called Indonesia, the Sultan had power over most of northern Borneo. Certain Dyak tribes of northern Borneo were among the most flagrant of the pirates. Local rulers made as much money out of owning pirate ships as they did out of ordinary trade. By 1830 the important men of Brunei were nearly all living off piracy, and the Sultan's honest advisers could not break their power.

At that time, the British, who had several trading bases in the South China Sea, were anxious to stamp out piracy. The British discovered that their steamships could chase and destroy the pirate galleys, while ordinary sailing ships could not.

British action thus brought an end to the worst of the piracy in northern Borneo, but it also weakened the state of Brunei. The Sultan was persuaded to give land to the successful pirate hunter, an Englishman named James Brooke. He was also persuaded to give other coastal land to the British government or to British companies. By 1880 Brunei had shrunk to its present size. By 1888 Brunei and the neighboring parts of northern Borneo were all under

In a system that has hardly changed for centuries, a bull provides the power for leveling a paddy field.

British rule. In 1946 those neighboring parts became British colonies; in 1963 they became part of Malaysia. Brunei did not wish to join Malaysia and remained separate. Modern Brunei is an independent country with a major oil industry.

WALLIS AND FUTUNA

These Polynesian islands lie in the central Pacific Ocean, northeast of Fiji. Wallis is one group of islands, and Futuna is the most important member of a group called the Hooru Isles. Wallis and Futuna became French dependencies in 1842, and together they now form an overseas territory of France. (See map on page 30.)

COMOROS

The Republic of the Comoros is a group of islands in the Indian Ocean. They lie between Africa and the northern point of Madagascar.

Comoros is comprised of three main islands. In the northwest is Njazidja, or Grande Comore, the biggest at 443 square miles (1,148 sq km). Njazidja has high volcanic mountains, including Mount Kartala, which is an active volcano. Njazidja also has miles of valuable forest.

In the south is Mwali, or Moheli, which is the smallest island. In the southeast is Nzwami, or Anjouan, a triangle of land rising to volcanic mountains in the middle.

The people are Malagasy, Arabs, and East Africans. Most live on lowlands near the coast of Njazidja and Nzwami. The climate is tropical and Comoros has a wet season, but in the center of the islands the rainwater soaks away through the volcanic rock. Only on the coastal lowlands can the people sink wells that will hold water. This is where they have always farmed.

Many of the people are of the same Malagasy tribes as those living in Madagascar. People have also migrated from Malaya, across the Indian Ocean. But the people who have probably affected the islands most are the Arabs.

The first European visitor came in about AD 1590. There he found Arab traders dealing in slaves and goods. The Arabs also brought with them their religion, Islam. The islands were part of an Arab trading network until the nineteenth century, and some of the present people are the descendants of the Arabs' African slaves.

In 1843 the French, who then held Madagascar, made the nearby island of Mayotte a French protectorate. In 1886 the Comoros islands were added to this protectorate. Under French rule big plantations were set up to grow cash crops. The French language came into use and took its place with Arabic and Swahili, an East African language, as a chief language of Comoros.

French rule ended in 1974, except in Mayotte, which chose to remain French. Comoros has since become independent as a republic, with Islam the state religion and Swahili the most common language. (See map on page 18.)

HONG KONG

Hong Kong is a small area on the coast of China, southeast of Canton. It has been under British rule since 1843. The colony of Hong Kong at first comprised just one island, called Hong Kong Island. But by 1860 both the peninsula of Kowloon and Stonecutters' Island were added to Hong Kong, and in 1898 the Chinese gave Britain a ninety-nine-year lease on 590 square miles (950 sq km). This area, then called the New Territory, makes up most of present Hong Kong, which is 665 square miles (1,065 sq km). Hong Kong is commercial and industrial, with over five million people, most of them Chinese. The area will become Chinese again in 1997. (See map on page 21.)

The top picture shows an ordination ceremony for Buddhist monks and nuns at a monastery.

A collection of motorized junks, houseboats, and floating restaurants in Aberdeen Harbor.

GLOSSARY

Aborigines: The earliest, primitive inhabitants of a country. The term is especially used in referring to the early Australians.

Atoll: An island bank of coral enclosing an area of shallow water.

Colony: A country or people ruled or settled by a foreign power.

Continent: One of the main divisions of land on this planet, such as Asia, Australia, or Europe.

Coral: The hard skeletons of various sea creatures that collectively, in the millions, often form reefs or islands in the sea.

Creole: A pidgin language in which French is one of the two languages.

Dependency: A country or territory with inadequate resources or defense that is entirely subject to the authority of a more powerful country.

Federation: A union of states that allow a central government some control over state matters.

Immigrants: People who enter a foreign country to live there permanently.

Melanesia: One of the three principal groups of Pacific islands (see map on page 30). The name means "black islands," and its peoples probably originally came from southeast Asia.

Micronesia: One of the three principal groups of Pacific islands (see map on page 30). The name means "small islands," and its peoples probably originally came from eastern Asia.

Missionaries: People whose job is to live in foreign lands and convert the people to their own religion.

Pidgin: A form of language in which the grammars of two or more languages are mixed together. Since pidgins usually appear in colonial countries, at least one language is that of the ruling country.

Polynesia: One of the three principal groups of Pacific islands (see map on page 30). The name means "many islands." The Polynesians have similar languages and cultures. We aren't certain how they reached the islands or where they came from, but they are probably from eastern Asia.

Protectorate: A weak state under the protection of a strong one that controls it wholly or partially.

Reef: A ridge of rocks or sand at or near the sea's surface.

Settlers: People who have come to a country to help develop it and to establish a new home for their descendants.

State: A country organized under a sovereign government. Also, a major area of such a country that decides state matters independently of other areas.

Sultan: The sovereign, or leader, of a Muslim country.

Territory: An area of land, usually separate from the main country, that is administered by an outside government. People from the territory are not part of the governing body.

World War I (1914-18): During this war, the Allies, including the United States and Canada, fought against the Germans in Europe and in northern Africa. At its conclusion, various German territories in the Far East and Pacific were handed over to one or the other of the victorious powers.

World War II (1939-45): During this war, the Allies fought against the Japanese in the Far East and the Pacific. At its conclusion Japan lost its overseas possessions.

Picture Acknowledgments — Alexander Turnbull Library, Wellington 52, 55; Australian Information Services 34-35, 46, 47 (upper); Australian Tourist Commission 47 (lower), cover (fourth picture); Author 7, 15, 26-27; Commonwealth Institute 8, 25, 36, 57; Consolidated Gold Fields 17; Government of Western Samoa 11; Hong Kong Government Office 61 (both); Hong Kong Tourist Board, cover (third picture); ICI 5; International Coffee Organization 33 (lower); Japan National Tourist Organization 40, 41, cover (first picture); F. Leather 42; Malaysian Rubber Research and Development Board 6; Mary Evans Picture Library 19, 20, 38, 51, 53; New South Wales Government 45; New Zealand National Publicity Studios 54, 56; A Shell Photograph 4, 22, 33 (upper), 59; State Electricity Commission of Victoria 44; The Tea Council 12-13; Tito Isola, University of the South Pacific 48; Tonga Visitors Bureau 28-29, 31.